WARTIME SPIES

CREATIVE EDUCATION • CREATIVE PAPERBACKS

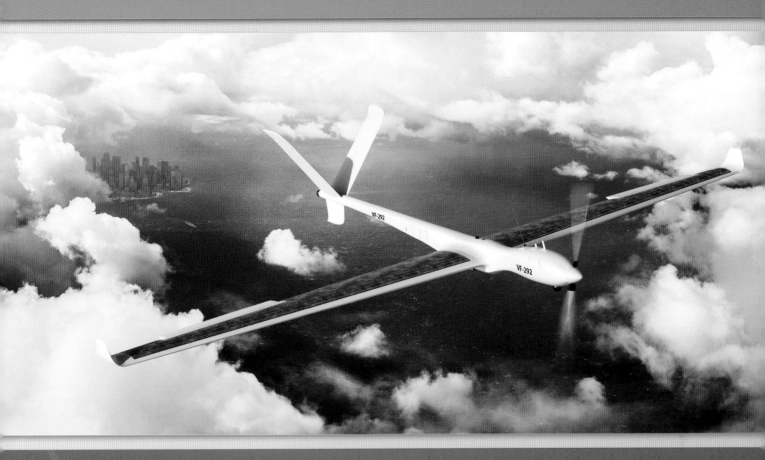

MODERN
SPIES

MICHAEL E. GOODMAN

Published by Creative Education and Creative Paperbacks
P.O. Box 227, Mankato, Minnesota 56002
Creative Education and Creative Paperbacks are imprints of
The Creative Company
www.thecreativecompany.us

Design and production by Chelsey Luther
Art direction by Rita Marshall
Printed in Malaysia

Photographs by Alamy (charistoone-images, epa european
pressphoto agency b.v., ZUMA Press Inc), AP Images (Christian
Charisius/picture-alliance/dpa, Brennan Linsley/ASSOCIATED
PRESS), Corbis (Arshad Arbab/epa, Colin Anderson/Blend Images,
David Bathgate, epa, Jason Hawkes, David Howells, Masatomo Kuri-
ya, Tim McConville, NASA/Science Photo Library, REUTERS TV/
Reuters, Savostyanov Sergei/ITAR-TASS Photo, Skyscan, Tim
Thompson, Viaframe, Markus von Luecken, PAUL WHITE/AP,
Stefan Zaklin/epa), Defense Video & Imagery Distribution System
(NASA), Dreamstime (Iulius Costache, Valentino Visentini), Getty
Images (EMMANUEL DUNAND, ATTA KENARE/AFP, John
Moore, Amy Sussman), Lost & Taken (Brant Wilson), Newscom (str
UPI Photo Service), TextureX.com (TextureX), VectorTemplates
.com

Library of Congress Cataloging-in-Publication Data
Goodman, Michael E.
Modern spies / Michael E. Goodman.
p. cm. — (Wartime spies)
Summary: An account of espionage during the modern age, including
famous spies such as Dayna Williamson Baer, covert missions, and
technologies that influence the course of present-day conflicts.
Includes bibliographical references and index.
ISBN 978-1-60818-600-6 (hardcover)
ISBN 978-1-62832-205-7 (pbk)
1. Intelligence service—United States—Juvenile literature. 2. United
States. Central Intelligence Agency—Juvenile literature. 3. Espionage, American—Juvenile literature. 4. Spies—United States—History—21st century—Juvenile literature. 5. Terrorism—Prevention—
Juvenile literature. I. Title.

JK468.I6G6643 2014
327.1273—dc23   2014037532

CCSS: RI.5.1, 2, 3, 5, 6, 8; RH.6-8.3, 4, 5, 6, 7, 8, 9

First Edition HC 9 8 7 6 5 4 3 2 1
First Edition PBK 9 8 7 6 5 4 3 2 1

CONTENTS

MOLE IN A CELL

On June 2, 2006, Canadian police conducted early-morning raids throughout the Toronto area. They arrested 13 adults and 4 teenagers, all members of a Muslim *terrorist cell* that the press began calling "The Toronto 17." The group planned to carry out a series of violent acts, including bombing the Toronto Stock Exchange and several government buildings. The police knew all about the group's plans because they had a *paid informant* working inside the cell, a devout Muslim named Mubin Shaikh. Shaikh kept his role as a spy very well hidden. He even helped the group get guns and taught members how to use the weapons. After the arrests, Shaikh explained why he agreed to become a *mole*. He didn't want innocent people to get hurt, and he hoped to prevent Toronto's peaceful Muslim community from being harshly criticized because of the group's actions. Some Canadian Muslims saw Shaikh as a hero; others considered him a traitor to his people.

TAKING *on* TERRORISTS

WITH THE COLLAPSE OF the Soviet Union in 1991, a long conflict known as the Cold War came to an end. The Cold War had pitted the United States and its close allies against the Soviet Union (as Russia was then known) and its allies for more than 40 years. It featured buildups of arms (including nuclear weapons), political challenges around the world, and lots of spying and *counterespionage*.

After the Cold War ended, there was a brief period of peace. Then new types of conflicts began, and new enemies emerged. In the Middle East and Central Asia, where most people practice Islam (the Muslim religion), groups of *extremists* began demanding that people follow stricter religious rules. Some extremist groups, such as the Taliban in Afghanistan, took control over national governments. Other groups carried out acts of violence against those they saw as enemies to

The two towers struck by planes on September 11 were part of a seven-building complex.

Islam. One especially violent Islamic group known as al-Qaeda targeted the U.S. and its institutions. First, al-Qaeda terrorists attacked U.S. *embassies* in Africa in 1998, killing more than 200 Americans and Africans. Next, they bombed a U.S. warship harbored in Yemen. Then on September 11, 2001 (often called "9/11"), a group of al-Qaeda-trained terrorists *hijacked* three planes and crashed them into the World Trade Center in New York and the Pentagon in Washington, D.C. They killed themselves and nearly 3,000 other people. Another plane, intended possibly for the White House, crashed in Pennsylvania when passengers fought with the hijackers. Nine days later, U.S. president George W. Bush spoke before a joint session of Congress and declared a "war on terror." He said the war would begin with al-Qaeda but would not end there. The U.S. would use its military power and its *intelligence* networks to "pursue nations that provide aid or safe haven to terrorism." Fighting such a war would require using both modern espionage tools and old-fashioned spying techniques.

COVERT OPS
ANIMAL SPIES

In July 2007, Iranian security police announced they had captured 14 spies attempting to race across the border between Iraq and Iran. The "spies" were squirrels. The police claimed that listening devices had been implanted in the squirrels to enable them to eavesdrop inside Iran. No other country claimed responsibility for sending in the squirrel spies, and the police provided no other details. This would not have been the first time animals were used for spying. Pigeons carried messages during World War I, and the U.S. Navy currently trains dolphins to sweep for mines and carry underwater cameras.

CHAPTER ONE

SPYING
in the 21ST
CENTURY

SPIES HAVE ALWAYS PLAYED an important role in wartime. Today, spies are active in peacetime, too, uncovering or protecting secrets. More than 2,000 years ago, a Chinese warrior and philosopher named Sun Tzu wrote, "Be subtle, be subtle, and use your spies for every kind of business." Sun Tzu could not have imagined the kinds of "businesses" that modern spies have to deal with. One area involves opposing terrorist groups such as al-Qaeda or nations believed to pose a threat to world peace when they engage in such activities as testing nuclear weapons. Some modern spies also focus on carrying out or preventing industrial espionage, the act of stealing company secrets from competing companies. Industrial espionage costs companies billions of dollars each year. A third modern spying concern involves protecting one's country from cyber espionage, or computer attacks by *hackers* trying to discover vital political and economic secrets. In the 2010s, for example, hackers based in China and Iran posed significant threats to the U.S. government and major American companies.

As part of the War on Terror, spies have tapped phones, implanted devices into computers, filmed secret meetings, intercepted and

Political leaders such as Iran's Ali Khamenei (above) know the value of Sun Tzu's (opposite) advice.

Some UAVs may also be referred to as remotely piloted or unmanned combat air vehicles.

analyzed electronic messages, and helped direct attacks by unmanned aerial vehicles (UAVs or "drones"). They have also carried out the kinds of tasks spies took on in earlier wars—breaking codes, recruiting local *assets*, planting moles inside enemy groups or facilities, and helping uncover or stop enemy spies.

Modern spies have a wide range of tools available, with new ones being invented almost every year. Still, at the core of all spy work are humans. *Operatives* for organizations such as the Central Intelligence Agency (CIA) in the U.S., the SVR in Russia, or the Mossad in Israel search for secrets themselves, or they recruit foreign assets to carry out espionage in their own countries. This type of spying is called HUMINT (human intelligence). HUMINT involves spies using their five senses and tools designed to enhance those senses. Some examples are night-vision goggles that enable activity in the dark or bugging devices capable of eavesdropping on conversations.

Actually, most spies today spend more time recruiting and directing others to do the "inside" work than taking photos, stealing documents, or planting bugs themselves. Think about spy television shows such as *Covert Affairs*. In almost every episode, CIA *agent* Annie Walker seeks out "locals" in foreign countries to find the information the CIA needs. That doesn't mean that her work isn't dangerous or that she doesn't have to do a lot of creative storytelling to deceive others. When they're on assignment, spies such as Annie generally don't use their own names or reveal for whom they work. They make up an identity called a cover. The cover needs to be realistic enough to fool police or counterintelligence agents in the foreign country. A blown cover can lead to arrest and a long prison term or even to being killed.

Former CIA agent Dayna Williamson Baer described a time her cover was almost blown while on assignment in the Mediterranean country of Cyprus. "I was parked only five minutes when a cop pulled up behind me.... I had a map on the passenger seat. Didn't I look like a tourist? He asked me if I'd accompany him to the station. I didn't have a choice. There he wrote down my name and passport

Using night-vision goggles helps military or intelligence forces maintain a cloak of secrecy.

13

number [both false] and asked why I was in Cyprus. I told him I was a film scout. I expected he'd ask what studio I worked for or something. (I had a story for that.) But he didn't, and he let me go. Anyhow, it spooked me, and now I try to spend the least time I need to on the street."

Although some espionage involves spies

Multinational company Unilever makes products from food and beverages to personal care items.

working undercover in foreign countries to learn military or government secrets, other espionage involves competing businesspeople. The simplest way to steal a competitor's secrets is to hire away one of its top employees and encourage the person to reveal confidential information. That happened in 2009, when two executives from Starwood Hotels joined Hilton

Hotels and brought along "truckloads" of secret documents with them that described the inner workings of Starwood's "W" chain of luxury hotels. Starwood successfully sued Hilton, which was ordered to pay a large sum to Starwood as damages and not allowed to create a competing chain of hotels for several years.

No spies were involved in the Starwood-Hilton situation, but they were in 2001 when Proctor and Gamble (P&G) attempted to steal secrets from its competitor Unilever. Among other actions, P&G's spies were caught going through Unilever's garbage dumpsters, looking for documents that might give away secrets. Other P&G spies posed as market analysts from a consulting group so that they could "interview" Unilever employees about sensitive topics. "Dumpster diving" and fake meetings are not the only techniques industrial spies use. Another method involves setting up false employment interviews and then taking pictures with hidden cameras or trying to sneak into computer files while visiting the company. Spies might also pose as repair workers or cleaning persons (such people almost seem invisible in an office) and plant bugs, view papers left on desks, or break into computers when no one is paying attention to them. More sophisticated industrial spies use cyber espionage. They hack into companies' e-mail accounts or computer networks to steal information.

The uptick in industrial espionage in

COVERT OPS
THE DOMES OF MENWITH HILL

The communications monitoring station at Menwith Hill in North Yorkshire, England, is one of the world's strangest-looking structures. Located on 545 acres (221 ha) of farmland, the station includes several large buildings and 33 radar domes that look like giant golf balls. The satellite receivers inside the domes can intercept 2 million communications per hour from around the world. Most of Menwith Hill's 1,800 employees are Americans connected to the National Security Agency (NSA). About 400 are Britons employed by their country's NSA counterpart. The hectic spy work going on inside Menwith Hill doesn't seem to bother the hundreds of sheep that calmly graze nearby.

The Menwith Hill domes are part of a British Royal Air Force station whose land is leased to the U.S.

15

modern times has also led to the creation of hundreds of new companies that help clients protect themselves from spying. Two examples are Murray Associates and Kaspersky Lab. Murray Associates has published a list of "Ten Spy-Busting Secrets" on its website for clients to follow. Suggestions include: (1) shred or destroy all waste paper and never store confidential documents in a cardboard box under a desk; (2) check credentials and work orders of anyone doing work in an office; (3) check locks and alarm systems regularly; (4) create long and complicated passwords to protect computers and e-mail accounts; and (5) make sure that employees do not leave confidential paperwork on their desks overnight. Kaspersky Lab also offers advice on its website and has posted a detailed report online entitled "Who's Spying on You?" that focuses on cyber espionage and how to deal with it.

Cyber spies don't attack only companies. Computer hacking and other types of long-range spying by foreign agents are also troublesome to governments around the world. For example, in May 2014, the U.S. Department of Homeland Security announced that it was investigating a series of attacks carried out between 2011 and 2014 by hackers from Iran, a country that has had government disputes with the U.S. The hackers sent e-mails to military contractors, government workers, and even members of Congress using addresses they might recognize. The messages contained computer viruses or fake login screens designed to steal usernames and passwords. Somehow, the attack went unnoticed for almost three years before a computer security firm hired by the U.S. government discovered and stopped what was going on. The hackers wanted to learn key government secrets. They also wanted to get revenge for a computer virus that the U.S. and Israel had installed at an Iranian nuclear plant to halt Iran's progress in developing potential nuclear weapons. For modern spies, computers can be a dangerous tool indeed.

The opening of nuclear power plants in Iran concerns some who think weaponization would follow.

CHAPTER TWO
TECHINT TOOLS *and* TROUBLES

FOR SOME SPYING ACTIVITIES, human senses—even aided by computers—are not enough; more technical tools are required. Intelligence gathered using technical tools is called TECHINT. There are specialized areas of TECHINT. IMINT (image intelligence) and PHOTINT (photographic intelligence) involve obtaining and studying images from cameras placed inside satellites, high-altitude airplanes, or UAVs. Some of the images are photographic; others, such as those transmitted by spy satellites orbiting in space, are digital. The cameras on modern satellites are so powerful that it is possible to read the numbers on a license plate from a vantage point 300 miles (483 km) above the earth.

UAVs are the newest IMINT tools for spying. Some are also used as weapons. The best-known *reconnaissance* drones are the Scout and Pioneer, first developed by Israeli scientists in the 1970s and '80s. The lightweight craft resemble gliders. They are directed by a pilot on the ground using a control panel. Pioneer drones can fly as fast as 90 miles (145 km) per hour at an altitude of up to 12,000 feet (3,658 m). Their small size and quick movements make them hard for enemies to shoot down. The drone pilot directs the craft with control instruments

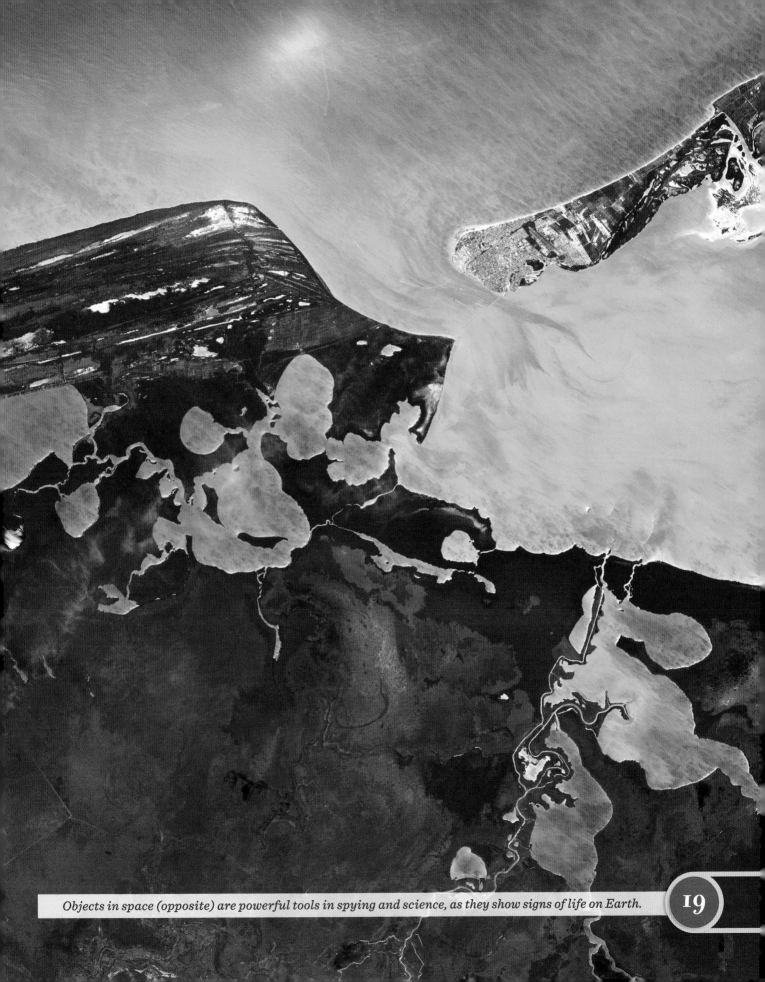

Objects in space (opposite) are powerful tools in spying and science, as they show signs of life on Earth.

19

just as a pilot on a full-size plane would. A remotely controlled zoom camera is attached to the bottom of the UAV. It can transmit live video during the day and *infrared* images during night missions.

Following the 9/11 terrorist attacks, the CIA began using armed UAVs called Predators against the Taliban and al-Qaeda in Afghanistan. Explosives from the drones caused damage and aroused fear, but they did not always hit their targets. One controversial attack occurred on February 4, 2002. The target was Osama bin Laden, the leader of al-Qaeda, who was believed to be hiding in Afghanistan. Several people were killed in the attack, but none of them was bin Laden. Instead, they were civilians gathering scrap metal on the ground. Since that time, Predators have been used effectively to strike terrorist leaders in different parts of the world. But many people object to the weapons because they often mistakenly harm civilians as well as terrorists.

Drones are not the only IMINT tools that have caused problems for the U.S. In May 1960, a CIA plane known as the U-2, flying at nearly 70,000 feet (21,336 m) over the Soviet Union, was shot down. The pilot, Francis Gary Powers, was supposed to destroy the plane and kill himself to avoid capture. He was unable to do either. After he parachuted to the ground, he was surrounded. Powers was tried and imprisoned as a spy. He was later exchanged for a Russian spy being held in a U.S. prison. The U.S. was also forced to admit that it was spying illegally over another country.

More than 40 years later, on April 1, 2001, a U.S. Navy EP-3E ARIES spy plane on an IMINT mission off the coast of China collided with a Chinese fighter plane closely following it. The Chinese plane crashed into the sea, killing the pilot, as the American aircraft began losing altitude. The American pilot was able to land safely on Hainan, a nearby Chinese island. As the plane tumbled, crew members didn't panic. They busily destroyed computer software and data files onboard that might have revealed the plane's spying activities. Chinese counterintelligence officers interrogated the 24-member American crew and then released them after 11 days. The Chinese kept the plane for two months to study its secrets. The U.S. temporarily stopped spying on

Predator drones have
been used in combat
situations since 1995
and can be equipped
to fire missiles.

China after the incident, but it resumed again several weeks later.

IMINT tools are used for visual spying. Two other related TECHINT areas—COMINT (communications intelligence) and SIGINT (signals intelligence)—involve intercepting, decoding, and analyzing communications. These communications can take the form of coded telegraph messages, radio signals, phone calls, e-mails, faxes, or Internet broadcasts. The U.S. intelligence agency that specializes in COMINT and SIGINT is the National Security Agency, or NSA. The NSA is America's largest and fastest-growing intelligence group, employing as many as 50,000 men and women. In addition, a number of private companies operate their own satellites and tracking devices and sell their services to the U.S. and to other governments.

Other countries have their own counterparts to the NSA. In Great Britain, the Government Communications Headquarters (GCHQ) maintains one of the world's most sophisticated communications monitoring systems at a center known as Menwith Hill. Russia has the Federal Security Service (FSB), Canada has the Communications Security Establishment Canada (CSEC), and France has the Directorate-General for External Security (DGSE).

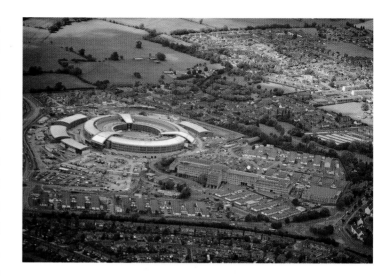

Nicknamed "The Doughnut," GCHQ's base is a circular building home to almost 6,000 employees.

The NSA was formed in 1952 and played a key role during the Cold War, tracking communications from the Soviet Union and its allies. It has also been actively involved in the War on Terror. However, the agency has received a lot of criticism in recent years for the quantity of communications it intercepts daily (about 1.7 billion e-mails, phone calls, and other types of communications) and the large number of people, companies, and organizations it tracks. Some lawmakers and business leaders have complained that NSA actions excessively invade Americans' privacy. U.S. military and intelligence leaders defend the NSA. They insist that its work is vital to protecting the country from enemies planning deadly attacks. In fact, the NSA has claimed that its wide-ranging surveillance programs

COVERT OPS
CLOTHING WARS

The business of designer clothing can be cutthroat. New and original fashion designs can bring in lots of money. That is why companies sometimes resort to industrial espionage to learn all they can about a competitor's new line of clothing. They may bribe dress cutters or seamstresses in a competing firm to copy and deliver patterns for items that are not yet ready for sale. They may also send in spies posing as fashion reporters to take photos or make sketches of the new designs. Then they can quickly produce their own copies, saving themselves money and cutting into the original designers' profits.

Fashion designers such as Tony Ward exhibit their dress collections at shows worldwide.

have helped prevent potential terrorist attacks on more than 50 occasions since 9/11.

Debate over the NSA's work made big headlines starting in June 2013. That was when Edward Snowden, a computer specialist working for a private company contracted by the NSA, released more than a million confidential documents to several media outlets. Snowden's actions were against the law. When he was hired, Snowden signed a form promising he wouldn't share confidential information, but he did so anyway. He said the public needed to know that the U.S. and other countries were engaged in what he thought were disturbing surveillance programs around the globe. For example, a program called PRISM allows the NSA or GCHQ (with pre-approval from courts) to collect and store individuals' Internet records and communications without their permission. Snowden alleged that the NSA's PRISM spying was so widespread that it was even tracking the mobile phone of Germany's chancellor (head of government) Angela Merkel. Merkel quickly demanded an explanation and an apology from U.S. president Barack Obama.

The information Snowden leaked caused a major stir in the U.S. and around the world. Many people were outraged, like Merkel, that their privacy was being invaded. Others said they were willing to give up some of their privacy if it meant that terrorists might be located and stopped.

Before he released the documents, Snowden fled to Hong Kong and then to Moscow, the capital of Russia. Snowden feared that if he returned to the U.S., he might be tried for treason and possibly executed. He insisted that he was not a traitor. Instead, he billed himself as a "whistleblower"—someone who exposes misconduct by a government or organization. He sought and was granted temporary *asylum* by the Russians and did not know if he would ever return to the U.S.

In August 2014, Russia gave Edward Snowden an official residency permit good for three years.

CHAPTER THREE

DO WOMEN MAKE *the* BEST SPIES?

IN AN INTERVIEW PRESENTED on the *Today* show in November 2013, reporter Ann Curry revealed a surprising statistic: Nearly half of the approximately 20,000 CIA employees were women. In fact, five of the top eight administrative positions at the agency—those who run departments—are held by women, including deputy director Avril D. Haines, the second-in-command. She meets with the U.S. president nearly every day to discuss security and intelligence issues.

Not only are women taking on more leadership roles, but the percentage of female agents in the field has also increased. Why are women assuming greater responsibilities in the intelligence business today? In September 2012, *Forbes* magazine suggested answers to that question in an article entitled "Why the Best Spies in Mossad and the CIA Are Women." The article suggested several reasons why women may be better suited to spying than men: (1) They have better "people skills." They make friends more easily than men and are better able to read people and see their strengths and weaknesses. Such a skill is essential in recruiting assets. (2) They have better "street smarts." Women are used to observing their surroundings carefully to see if someone potentially dangerous is following them. (3) Women have a

Although women bring valuable skills to spy work, the media usually emphasizes their looks instead.

"nurturing instinct." They generally take better care of their assets than men do. (4) Women are better listeners, which also helps them handle their assets better. The article included an interview with the head of the Mossad who stated that women are better at multitasking (doing several things at the same time) than men and better able to make up new identities.

Few women played leading intelligence roles at the CIA when it was first established in 1947. Back then, the agency hired many female employees, but they were mostly secretaries or assistants. That was still true until the late 1970s. Then agency leaders began focusing on building "woman-power" within the

Valerie Plame Wilson spent almost two decades with the CIA until her cover was blown.

CIA. A memo sent to male senior leaders asked, "What kind of careers do you want for [your daughters] in the CIA? Do you want to see their opportunities limited to the [low levels] where the majority of women in the Agency remain today?" The memo seemed to have an impact. Women have been making a steady rise within the CIA since the 1980s, both as administrators and as *case officers* for covert operations (undercover activities).

Most women employed by the CIA or other American intelligence agencies today work in offices or laboratories—doing research, analyzing data, writing reports, or developing new spy equipment. The small percentage who work as spies in the field often have to keep their identities unknown and their work a secret, even from their closest relatives. That was how Lindsay Moran and Dayna Williamson Baer lived when they served as CIA operatives in the 1990s and 2000s. Each handled hair-raising undercover assignments in Eastern Europe. After they decided to leave the agency (for different reasons), they wrote books to share their experiences with the world.

Moran described her background, CIA training, and spying activities in *Blowing My Cover: My Life as a CIA Spy*. She explained that, growing up, she always wanted to be a spy. She read spy books, shared coded messages with her friends, and even packed her suitcase in special ways when traveling, so she could see if

A NEW USE FOR SPY SATELLITES

During the Cold War, the U.S. put spy satellites into orbit to monitor nuclear weapons development and testing sites. Starting in the 1990s, some of these satellites were tasked with locating factories in South America producing illegal drugs and the routes used for transporting drugs past enforcement agents. Most of the reconnaissance work was kept secret because American CIA and Drug Enforcement Agency (DEA) officials didn't want to let the drug runners know what was going on. "Everybody knows the satellites are up there, and knows they help things," one DEA official said. "But we don't like to talk about it."

Coast Guard and other military personnel often assist in seizing materials for DEA cases.

anyone had searched her belongings. While in college, she developed a special interest in Eastern Europe and taught English in Bulgaria for a while. Then she applied for a job with the CIA. After going through several interviews and a lie-detector test, she was accepted. She began a yearlong training program at Camp Peary, located near Williamsburg, Virginia. CIA agents call it "The Farm."

As part of her training, she learned and practiced special spy skills called tradecraft. These tactics included learning how to develop a cover; how to avoid being followed; how to mingle comfortably at parties and in the streets with potential local assets; and how to set up a *dead drop* for collecting intelligence from assets. She also practiced some unusual skills that came in handy later on the job—how to drive cars fast, how to write notes while driving, and how to look calm all the while so that someone following her wouldn't know she was aware of being tailed.

Moran didn't always like her work as a case officer. She eventually decided to resign from the agency in 2003 after five years on the job. She said, "It's a dirty business because you're lying to people and you're using them, and that's what your job is. That's the reality of being a spy. You're not befriending people because you like them or because you want to be friends with them; you think that they have some information that will be of value to the U.S. government."

Dayna Williamson joined the CIA out of graduate school in 1991. She thought working for the agency would be a great adventure. While in training at The Farm, she discovered she was an exceptional shot on the rifle range. Once she became an agent, she was invited to attend a basic training course for bodyguards and shooters. "It was six months of grueling day-and-night drilling in pistols, shotguns, automatic weapons, hand-to-hand combat, high-speed driving, and killing someone by shoving a pencil up through their hard palate [roof of the mouth]," she said.

SPY

Lindsay Moran wanted to expose the more "dys-functional" aspects of the CIA in her book.

She completed the training and then went on missions in different parts of the world. The work was dangerous but exciting. However, being away from home for long periods and having to be so secretive about her whereabouts eventually caused so much strain in her marriage that she got divorced.

A few years later, she was on assignment in Sarajevo, the capital of Bosnia and Herzegovina in southeastern Europe. Her new partner was a veteran CIA operative named Robert Baer, who had also gotten divorced while working for the agency. They worked together well and were attracted to each other, but they knew how difficult it was to juggle marriage and spy work. Eventually, they decided to leave the CIA before getting married again. It wasn't an easy decision for either partner. "At first, I felt lost," Dayna said. "But I knew that life with Bob would never be dull." In 2011, the couple wrote a book about their adventures in the CIA entitled *The Company We Keep*.

Thanks to their first-person accounts, we know a lot about Moran and Williamson Baer. However, another famous CIA operative from the 2000s remains anonymous. She spent five years leading the mission to locate bin Laden, which ended with his death on May 2, 2011, in Abbottabad, Pakistan. The agent's role in the search for and capture of bin Laden was dramatized in the 2012 movie *Zero Dark Thirty*, in which she was called Maya. Maya's best quality was her determination and refusal to give up the search, even when it seemed to be futile. Her true identity has not been revealed because she is still an active spy. For spies in the field, their security demands anonymity. If Maya's cover were blown, she might easily become a terrorist target.

The 2005 film Syriana *was based on the experiences of and books by Robert Baer (above).*

CHAPTER FOUR

TRUE TALES
from the WAR
on TERROR

A **TTACKS BY MODERN TERRORISTS** differ from those carried
out in earlier wars. Today's attackers use deadly weapons, from
guns and bombs to toxic chemical and biological substances, and they
don't seem to care if their weapons harm civilians in addition to sol-
diers. In fact, that seems to be their motive in many cases. Some terrorists, such as those who struck on 9/11, are also willing to blow
themselves up to achieve maximum damage. That makes them even
more dangerous. An enemy who doesn't value his own life is hard to
win over with threats or bribes.

While the types of attacks conducted by terrorists may be new,
some of the espionage methods for battling terrorists are similar to
those used in earlier conflicts. These include placing moles inside terrorist cells, bribing informants, and carrying out quick and sometimes
deadly counterattacks. Without an end in sight, though, such measures and countermeasures could drag on and on.

One of the low points for the CIA in the War on Terror involved a
surprise attack by a suicide bomber. It occurred on December 30,
2009, inside a military outpost in Afghanistan. One victim was a CIA

Violent retaliatory measures (opposite) and suicide bombings (above) are all too frequent occurrences.

35

analyst from Rockford, Illinois, named Elizabeth Hanson. Hanson was not a field operative, but she still had to keep her mission secret. She was part of a team working on a major breakthrough against al-Qaeda. The team had been in close contact with a Jordanian doctor who was a mole inside an al-Qaeda cell. The doctor said he had information on how to locate bin Laden's second-in-command and possibly bin Laden himself. He needed to give his report in person so that there would be no possibility of having a radio or e-mail communication intercepted.

The doctor drove his own car to the border between Pakistan and Afghanistan. Then he was transported to the outpost by a CIA security officer. Hanson would be in charge of *debriefing* him. The meeting was so important that even the White House had been alerted. The CIA vehicle passed through several security checkpoints, and a second car escorted it to a small building where Hanson and her boss were waiting to question the doctor. The doctor got out of the car. Then he started to pray while keeping one hand inside his pants pocket. A security guard asked the doctor to remove his hand so that he could be searched. Suddenly, the

doctor pushed something that triggered a hidden bomb strapped to his chest. The explosion sent thousands of steel pellets flying through the air, killing everyone nearby, including Hanson.

It would be several days before Hanson's family and friends learned of her death. Some were surprised to learn that she was on the front lines in the War on Terror. A year later, a star was carved into the CIA's Memorial Wall at the agency's Virginia headquarters honoring her service to her country.

The Jordanian doctor's deception—tricking the CIA into believing he was a mole helping the agency—cost several American lives. More than a decade earlier, the CIA had been deceived by perhaps the trickiest al-Qaeda *double agent* of all, a former Egyptian army captain named Ali Abdul Saoud

A video released January 9, 2010, seemed to link the Jordanian doctor (right) to the Taliban.

DON'T SWAT THAT FLY!

In 2001, Harvard University engineering professor Robert Wood began creating a mini-UAV that looks and acts like a housefly. After 12 years, he came up with a model light enough to fly around while being controlled electronically by a human on the ground. The man-made insect has tiny wings that can flap 120 times a second. It is equipped with a sensor that can record visual images. American intelligence agencies hope this "robo-insect" can be a spy of the future. Wood believes his invention can have other valuable uses, such as locating missing people at disaster sites or tracking air pollutants.

Scientists who develop mini-UAVs are increasingly inspired by real flying creatures.

Mohamed (Ali Mohamed, for short). He did such a good job of deceiving the American intelligence leaders who employed him that his al-Qaeda associates called him Ali Amiriki ("Ali the American").

Mohamed first offered his services to the CIA in 1984 in Cairo, Egypt. CIA leaders suspected that he might be an Egyptian spy, but they still assigned him some minor tasks. Somehow, he found his way to the U.S., where he began working as an adviser first for the American army and then for the Federal Bureau of Investigation (FBI) and the CIA. Mohamed offered to help the FBI in its counterintelligence efforts against suspected Muslim terrorists in the U.S. What he was really doing was using his FBI contacts to find information to help the terrorists. Over the next several years, he often traveled between California and the Middle East. It is not clear why the CIA never stopped him during any of these trips nor ever suspected that he might be a double agent for al-Qaeda. During the trips, he helped train al-Qaeda forces, including bin Laden, based in Afghanistan. Then he helped plan the deadly attacks on U.S. embassies in Kenya and Tanzania in 1998.

The FBI finally began focusing on Mohamed after the embassy bombings. He was arrested and pled guilty to conspiracy to kill American nationals living outside the U.S. What happened next is still a mystery. Mohamed was never formally sentenced for his crimes. Instead, he made a deal offering to provide information about al-Qaeda, including how to find its leaders in Afghanistan. His inside information became even more valuable after the 9/11 attacks. It is possible that he was given a new identity as part of the Witness Security Program (WITSEC). An American journalist named Peter Lance has written a book about Mohamed called *Triple Cross* that reveals some of the mysteries surrounding the remarkable spy.

The CIA was more successful in capturing the possible mastermind of the 9/11 attacks, Khalid Sheikh Mohammed (often called

The simultaneous 1998 bombings in East African cities were carried out by explosive-laden trucks.

39

"KSM"). After the 9/11 attacks, KSM went into hiding in Pakistan. The CIA partnered with Pakistan's Inter-Services Intelligence (ISI) on an intense hunt for him. Exactly one year after 9/11, ISI and CIA operatives raided a group of apartments in the capital city of Karachi. Several people were arrested, but KSM escaped.

The near miss made CIA agents even more determined. They located a Pakistani man who knew KSM well and bribed him to make contact with his friend. It took four months and many bribes, but finally, on February 28, 2003, a CIA agent received the text message, "I am with KSM." At 2:00 the following morning, ISI and CIA agents raided the apartment in Rawalpindi where KSM was hiding and placed him under arrest. According to reports about the raid, a CIA agent rumpled KSM's hair before taking his photo so that he would look unattractive and evil. That picture of KSM soon appeared in newspapers and Internet news bulletins around the world.

The story of KSM doesn't end there, though. While his capture was a bright moment for the U.S. in the War on Terror, his imprisonment and subsequent interrogation have led to new problems. KSM was flown to an American military prison called Guantánamo on the island of Cuba. He claimed that he was tortured into providing information about al-Qaeda. The torture possibly included a process known as "waterboarding"—pouring water over someone's face to make him feel as though he is drowning. The technique is not permitted by international rules of treatment for prisoners of war. U.S. military officials at Guantánamo denied the allegations. Still, the accusations upset people around the world and spurred a larger conversation over the treatment of prisoners—especially those known to be terrorists.

The detainment area
constructed in 2002 at
Guantánamo Bay, Cuba,
was named Camp Delta.

A WAR
without END

MANY AMERICANS HAD HOPED the 2011 Abbottabad raid that ended in the death of al-Qaeda leader Osama bin Laden would break up the organization and end the War on Terror. The raid was the culmination of 10 years of effort not only by members of the CIA and NSA in America but also by intelligence groups in other countries. While the hunt for bin Laden involved using many of the most sophisticated spying tools available, the terrorist leader was brought down thanks to a heavier reliance on HUMINT tools rather than TECHINT. Nervous that electronic communications might be intercepted, bin Laden had always insisted on all messages to him being delivered in person by a courier. So the real hunt involved identifying and

Apart from the loss of life and property, the 2004 Madrid train bombings affected Spanish politics.

following the courier. That was the main task that "Maya" and her CIA team set out to accomplish. And it worked!

Even while intelligence forces were hunting for bin Laden, numerous other deadly terrorist attacks were going on around the world in the 2000s. In Moscow, in October 2002, a group of 40 terrorists from Chechnya on the Russian border took more than 800 people hostage in a movie theater. Russian police used chemical gases to kill the terrorists, but 130 hostages died as well. In Madrid, Spain, on March 11, 2004, terrorists set off bombs in commuter trains that killed 191 people and wounded 1,800. In London, on July 7, 2005, terrorists detonated four bombs inside the city's subway system and a double-decker bus. The explosions killed 52 people and injured 700 others. Numerous attacks and suicide bombings in Israel and other Middle Eastern countries have become so commonplace that people almost expect them to occur. No one is sure when, or if, the war being waged by terrorists or the War on Terror opposing them will ever come to an end.

COVERT OPS
FIVE EYES

During World War II, five English-speaking nations decided to combine their SIGINT capabilities for certain projects. The group known as the "Five Eyes" was made up of Australia, Canada, New Zealand, the United Kingdom (Great Britain), and the U.S. The name was short for "AUS/CAN/NZ/UK/US EYES ONLY," which was often printed at the top of classified communications among the group. The Five Eyes continued to work together in the 2000s, utilizing a network known as ECHELON that enables them to spy on Internet communications around the world. Some people have criticized the Five Eyes for invading people's privacy, but the allies have not allowed such complaints to deter their surveillance work.

MODERN SPIES

TIMELINE

FEBRUARY 26, 1993 — Muslim extremists set off a bomb in the basement of the World Trade Center in New York City, killing 6 and injuring more than 1,000 others.

FEBRUARY 23, 1998 — Al-Qaeda declares war on the U.S. and its supporters.

AUGUST 7, 1998 — Al-Qaeda terrorists set off explosions in U.S. embassies in Kenya and Tanzania.

APRIL 1, 2001 — A U.S. Navy spy plane collides with a Chinese fighter jet. The Chinese pilot dies, and the American crew is held by the Chinese for 11 days.

SEPTEMBER 11, 2001 — Al-Qaeda-trained terrorists hijack American aircraft and crash them into the World Trade Center in New York and the Pentagon in Washington, D.C.

SEPTEMBER 20, 2001 — U.S. president George W. Bush declares a "war on terror."

SEPTEMBER 28, 2001 — The United Nations Security Council passes Resolution 1373, calling on all nations to work together to fight terrorism.

OCTOBER 7, 2001 — American forces begin fighting against the Taliban in Afghanistan.

OCTOBER 26, 2001 — The U.S. Patriot Act is passed, giving the government and American intelligence services increased powers to search for and arrest terrorist suspects.

JANUARY 11, 2002 — The first captured terrorist suspects are held at the Guantánamo Bay prison camp in Cuba.

FEBRUARY 1, 2002

American journalist Daniel Pearl is kidnapped and executed by terrorists in Pakistan. Al-Qaeda member Khalid Sheikh Mohammed ("KSM") later admits to beheading Pearl.

MARCH 1, 2003

KSM is arrested by Pakistani and American intelligence personnel in Rawalpindi, Pakistan. He is imprisoned at Guantánamo.

MARCH 20, 2003

A U.S.-led coalition of armed forces invades Iraq to force dictator Saddam Hussein out of power.

MARCH 11, 2004

Terrorists set off 10 bombs at almost the same time inside commuter trains in Madrid, Spain, killing 191 and injuring 1,800 others.

JULY 7, 2005

Four bombs are detonated inside London's subway system and a bus. The act of terrorism kills 52 people and injures 700 others.

JUNE 7, 2006

Abu Musab al-Zarqawi, the leader of al-Qaeda in Iraq, is killed by a U.S. air strike as he meets with other terrorists near Baqubah, Iraq.

AUGUST 5, 2009

The Taliban leader in Afghanistan, Baitullah Mehsud, is killed by an American Predator drone.

JANUARY 2010

An audiotape allegedly from Osama bin Laden claims responsibility for an attempt to blow up a plane en route to Michigan on Christmas Day 2009.

MAY 1-2, 2011

Bin Laden is found in Abbottabad, Pakistan, and killed by American special forces.

MAY 5, 2012

The trial of KSM and four other terrorist suspects officially begins at Guantánamo.

GLOSSARY

AGENT—a person who works for an intelligence service; a spy

ASSETS—local people acting as spies for a foreign agency or providing secret information to a spy

ASYLUM—protection given by a government to someone who has left another country in order to escape being arrested or harmed

CASE OFFICERS—intelligence officers who recruit agents and manage their activities; sometimes called "handlers"

COUNTERESPIONAGE—efforts made to prevent or block spying by an enemy

DEAD DROP—a secure location that usually includes a sealed container where spies and their handlers can exchange information or intelligence materials to avoid meeting in person

DEBRIEFING—questioning someone about a completed mission or undertaking

DOUBLE AGENT—a spy who pretends to work for one country or organization while acting on behalf of another

EMBASSIES—headquarters of ambassadors and staff in foreign countries

EXTREMISTS—people prepared to use extreme measures, including violence, to get what they want

HACKERS—people who use computers to gain unauthorized access to data

HIJACKED—illegally seized an aircraft, ship, or vehicle in transit and forced it to go to a different destination

INFRARED—seen under low-light conditions using devices that send out shortwave emissions

INTELLIGENCE—information of political or military value uncovered and transmitted by a spy

MOLE—an employee of one intelligence service who actually works for another service or who works undercover within the enemy group in order to gather intelligence

OPERATIVES—secret agents working for an intelligence group

PAID INFORMANT—a person who takes money to provide information to the police about secret or criminal activities

RECONNAISSANCE—scouting or exploring, often for a militaristic or strategic purpose

TERRORIST CELL—a group that works together to plan and carry out violent acts; in terrorist organizations, individual cells often work independently but share common goals

SELECTED BIBLIOGRAPHY

Aid, Mathew M. *Intel Wars: The Secret History of the Fight against Terror.* New York: Bloomsbury, 2012.

Baer, Robert B., and Dayna Baer. *The Company We Keep: A Husband-and-Wife True-life Spy Story.* New York: Crown, 2011.

Coleman, Janet Wyman. *Secrets, Lies, Gizmos, and Spies: A History of Spies and Espionage.* New York: Abrams Books for Young Readers, 2006.

Fridell, Ron. *Spying: The Modern World of Espionage.* Brookfield, Conn.: Twenty-First Century Books, 2002.

Kushner, Harvey W. *Encyclopedia of Terrorism.* Thousand Oaks, Calif.: Sage, 2003.

Moran, Lindsay. *Blowing My Cover: My Life as a CIA Spy.* New York: Putnam, 2005.

Owen, David. *Hidden Secrets.* Buffalo, N.Y.: Firefly Books, 2002.

Priest, Dana, and William M. Arkin. "Top Secret America: *A Washington Post* Investigation; Monitoring America." *Washington Post*, July 19–21, 2010. http://projects.washingtonpost.com/top-secret-america/articles.

WEBSITES

CIA JOB OPPORTUNITIES
https://www.cia.gov/careers/opportunities/cia-jobs
A description of career and internship opportunities in the various divisions of the CIA and requirements for applying for different jobs. A similar website describing employment at the National Security Agency (NSA) is available at *http://www.nsa.gov/careers/*.

CIA MUSEUM COLLECTION
https://www.cia.gov/about-cia/cia-museum/experience-the-collection/index.html
Stories, biographies, and a detailed timeline of events from the 1990s to the present.

INDEX